D0733887

SATELLITE

MATTHEW
R●HRER

SATELLITE

VERSE PRESS AMHERST, MA

Published by Verse Press

Copyright © 2001 by Verse Press
All rights reserved

Library of Congress Cataloging-in-Publication Data
Rohrer, Matthew.
  Satellite / Matthew Rohrer. — 1st ed.
     p. cm.
  ISBN 0-9703672-3-6
  I. Title.
  PS3568.052 s28 2001
  811'.54—dc21   00-013084

Printed in the United States of America

9 8 7 6 5 4 3 2 1

FIRST EDITION

Contents

Acknowledgments

I am grateful to the editors of the following journals for publishing these poems:

The Iowa Journal of Cultural Studies: Yes; Credo. *Faucheuse*: When Distance Began; Folklore. *The Iowa Review*: After the Wedding Party; Child's Lament Sung from a Rooftop; Joyfully, but Briefly; Starfish Waving to Me from the Sand. *Columbia Magazine*: The Amaranth. *Verse*: Beautiful Things; The End of Something Falls On a Tuesday; Fragment, with Golem; Like the Back of a Star; My Government; Cutting Through the Dark. *Seattle Review*: Mockingbirds. *The Boston Review*: Homage to My Waitress. *The Chicago Review*: Precision German Craftsmanship; Childhood Stories. *Conduit*: Philosophy in the Boudoir; Alternatives to Pain; The Bells. *Swerve*: Sonnets to Mayhem. *Nerve.com*: The Robotroid Girlfriend; Gliding Toward the Lamps. *New York Sidewalk.com*: Brooklyn Bridge.

After the Wedding Party also appeared in *Real Things: An Anthology of Postmodern American Poetry* (Indiana University Press).

Brooklyn Bridge; Precision German Craftsmanship; and Gliding Toward the Lamps appeared in *The New Young American Poets* (Southern Illinois University Press).

Comet; Starfish Waving to Me from the Sand; Childhood Stories; and Precision German Craftsmanship appeared in *The Breadloaf Anthology of New American Poets* (University Press of New England).

I would like to thank John Yau, David Shapiro and Susan McCullough, for their close and careful readings, and their encouragement. I would also like to thank Declan Patrick McManus and Robyn Hitchcock, for their Satellites.

for Susan

The worst imaginable kind of fascism would be
if the soul belonged only to the living,
and not to the dust and stones!

TOMAŽ ŠALAMUN

THE AMARANTH

is an imaginary flower that never fades.
The amaranth is blue with black petals,
it's yellow with red petals,
it's enormous and grows into the shape
of a girl's house,
the seeds nestle high in the closet
where she hid a boy.
The boy and his bike flee
the girl's parents from the tip
of the leaves, green summer light
behind the veins.
The amaranth is an imaginary flower
in the shape of a girl's house
dispensing gin and tonics
from its thorns, a succulent.
This makes the boy's bike steer
off-course all summer, following
the girl in her marvelous car,
the drunken bike.

He was a small part of summer,
he was summer's tongue.

CHILDHOOD STORIES

They learned to turn off the gravity in an auditorium
and we all rose into the air,
the same room where they demonstrated
pow-wows and prestidigitation.

But not everyone believed it.
That was the most important lesson
I learned — that a truck driven by a dog
could roll down a hill at dusk
and roll right off a dock into a lake
and sink, and if no one believes you
then what is the point
of telling them wonderful things?

I walked home from the pow-wow
on an early winter night in amazement:
they let me buy the toy tomahawk!
As soon as I got home I was going
to hit my sister with it, but I didn't know this.

PRECISION GERMAN CRAFTSMANSHIP

It was a good day and I was about to do something important
and good, but then I unscrewed the pen I was using
to see the ink. Precision German craftsmanship.
The Germans are so persnickety and precise,
they wash their driveways. Their mountains and streams
dance around each other in a clockwork, courtly imitation
of spring. They built the Panzer tank, out of rakes
hoses and garden gnomes; they built me.
And I've seated myself above an avenue on the brink
of mystery, always just on the lip, with my toes over the lip
but my bowels behind.

When I replaced the ink the sky was socked in,
only one window of blue open in the north, directly over someone.
But that person was reading about Rosicrucians in the laundromat,
he was unaware as the blue window closed above him.
The rest of us are limp and damp,
I see a button in front of us that says "spin cycle."
I'm going to push it.

17

PIG-IN-A-BLANKET

I wake up, bound tightly.
A warm, valerian smell cascades
to my palate. I can only move
my eyelids and toes.
Heat sits impishly on my chest,
at my throat, curtains of it brushing against me.
Panic creeps out of my armpits.
I can only move my eyelids and toes,
and this constant fluttering
lulls me to sleep.

I awake late and move like a bee
through the apartment,
from station to station
from the blue flame
to the shimmering disc.
From the stairs to the street,
to the grocery store.
To the meat aisle. To the cocktail wieners.
To make pigs-in-a-blanket,
to share them with friends.
To sink into bed, to bind myself
tightly in blankets, to flutter off into sleep,
and then on past sleep,
to be carried by admirers across a wooden bridge.
Later I will burn this bridge.

18

BENEATH THE WHEEL
OF A STUNT

Four boys lay in a row
in a pit, the class bully
on his dirt bike above them
passed through the sun
and emerged with the sun
stringing off him.

The boys pointed their bellies up
to the tops of the sweetgum trees
and to the wrinkled skin of the cottonwoods,
which peeled back in the bright light.
The bully's gnarled tires
spun backwards, madness.

The boys trembled
under their eyelids and in their duodena.
The sky lowered its blue eyes at one of them—
he prayed to grow older
and please women.

PHILOSOPHY
IN THE BOUDOIR

1.

A woman looks at the penis of a man she's known
for a long time. She thinks . . . nothing. But she feels
very warm. He feels happy, like everyone
is inspecting the painting he made at school.
Snow buffets under orange streetlights outside.
The rest is darkness. In the emptiness,
there is not even one idea.
That there are things standing outside emptiness,
like brick houses,
reassures the people who disrobe together and kneel
on top of the sheets inside them.

2.

The man is lying on top of the sheets listening to a song
replay in his memory.

He fools with it a little, like candy cooling.
The woman seems to be asleep.
The white thermal blanket across her haunches
slopes gently into the distance like a winter field
and rises rhythmically unlike one.
A black cat sleeps across an open dictionary.
He knows things we'll never know.

EPITHALAMIUM

In the middle garden is the secret wedding,
that hides always under the other one
and under the shiny things of the other one. Under a tree
one hand reaches through the grainy dusk toward another.
Two right hands. The ring is a weed that will surely die.

There is no one else for miles,
and even those people far away are deaf and blind.
There is no one to bless this.
There are the dark trees, and just beyond the trees.

REDUCED TO TEMPING

Some people are offensively timid.
When I stand near them, and if I
haven't seen any other people for weeks,
I feel like a star's bodyguard
and the timid person is an egg or worm.
Alone, I rush across
rainy sidewalks with no umbrella,
with my shoulders drawn in. My ribcage locked.
Something moves overhead at all times:
I am sometimes more, sometimes less, aware
of this looming constant. Lean your head back
and think about that for a few seconds:
you're very tiny, you're in outer space.
You see I'm right.

SUNDAY NIGHT

In the summers you crawled around
when I slept outside, where you slept.
You crawled around when I climbed the tower
and rolled back the canvas from its grommets
to watch stars falling
at One A.M., which was the time
set aside for shooting stars.
At One A.M. the stars shot each other
and some of them fell into the tops of the Sweetgum trees.

I brought you food, my sister's clothes
to dress you in, though I suspect you
only let me dress you because there was nothing
else you needed to do. Were you jealous?
When I made love with someone
in the garden and the moon reflected a suicide
on the train tracks across town,
you came to watch.
When the satellites trickled through the stars
like a pinball machine, you never spoke.
You never spoke. But you liked it
when I combed your hair.
It was always a Sunday night just before the end of school.

23

BEAUTIFUL THINGS

When we say something is beautiful
we mean we can laterally bisect it.
The moon for instance has the day side and the night.
A manta ray has two black wings.
A girl's face has one green eye, one nostril up-turned
like half a ski jump, 16 teeth,
and then again.
Elizabeth Taylor, the most symmetrical of us all.
A peach with two soft sides, two halves of a poisoned seed.

Even the five-pointed starfish fits into our group.
The best time to bisect a starfish is at night
after a shipwreck when they grip the shore.
They say they are the hands of sailors who didn't make it.

CHILD'S LAMENT SUNG
FROM A ROOFTOP

One ant switching from one blade of grass
to another, replicated a thousand times
in the sunny rectangle.
By the time the sunlight reaches us, it's in another form,
enormous blue particles.
By the time it reaches us, it's old, and we're old.
We're holding in our bladders with blue straps.
Grackles rise from tufts of grass into the light,
loving each other. Or doing something similar,
simply committing deeds under the sun,
one leading to the next, to a roof where a child laughs.
The child's ball has a propeller inside it, it lifts off,
it rises, the child realizes this might be his last chance
to say something to it.
Oh ball, you were the perfect toy.
When I reach puberty I will leave this rectangle
in search of a woman exactly like you.

PETITION FOR ABSOLUTION

I wanted to go down into the elevator shaft and try it again,
drop it a hundred times and see
if the lab monkey would fall through the space
between the elevator and the floor
as easily as it just had.
I always wanted to try out those percentage and number challenges
though I was a miserable math student
and took every problem personally. The monkey was dead,
or dead to us, who would never go into the shaft
looking for it. We knew too much:
escaped creatures, experimental ingots of amber resin,
and plenty of loose nuggets of lab chow
swept into the darkness when no one was looking.

●

Everything had to be done in a very particular way
which is how you know you're working for the government.
I had a map of the floor with a pattern in which it must be mopped.
I had a locker and in it my costume which I had to step into
then out of in reverse order for sterility.
I had a mask, ear plugs, gloves, and a pen and notebook
in which I was to record the first words
the lab animals said,
if that happened to be a side-effect of their treatment.

•

Worst was to hear the dogs but never see them.
The humidity on the tiles. The walls made of tiles,
the ceiling tiles conducting the dogs' beseeching perfectly.

•

After hours, anaesthetized rabbits
in the center of a sterile room.
I hid behind my moist mask,
having come to shake them awake
and read to them from my petition for absolution.

2

THE HUNGER
OF THE LEMUR

On a hill he had climbed all winter
the lemur noticed a small black bird
with yellow spots,
the way the night ought to look.

The hill still slept under his feet
like something hard and dead,
it was the birds who were different.
The large black ones, without confidence
now that the trees were softening
and the roofs warming up like pans.

A police car sighed with the contentment
of the overfed.
Burst chokecherries sat around
as reminders of death.
A girl stopped, then walked the other way.
The lemur couldn't smell anything besides himself
as if for the first time.
He thought:

I am a nose in a vacuum
shaped like a nose

I am the only lemur on the grey ice

These are only the slimy bones of trees,
not trees.

THE END OF SOMETHING FALLS ON A TUESDAY

The way the magpie is secretly green,
we stayed for dinner, we uncorked the wine.

In such a way that the wine disappeared quickly
in the half light, we dredged the bottle for solids.

They were like jewels, without the shapes.
In a room that opened onto a smaller room

where a deaf man's music struggled,
we spread out the solids on a low table.

A magpie wrestled twigs and a child's toy
into his home.

This was the perfect season for the evening,
evening's light dazzling our small black eyes.

Separated from the magpie by a pane of glass
and music coming down like a velvet curtain,

we could only imagine
the flavor of the evening's air.

DESIRE'S INTERIM

By holding your shoulders
at night I keep from sliding
out the bottom of the bed
and into the grey strands,
fingernails, our sheet's crumbs,
a dark place where no one belongs.

By resting my nose on the foothills
of your hairline I keep from slipping
out of our blue humidor
into the smell of stockings, to dust
myself off and stand above you,

while you are sunken. In the orange night
you are sunken as if into the beach after a storm.
There is a buried treasure nearby.
The map is drawn on the small of your back
by a boy straddling you. Rats are repelled
by the palm trees' metal bands. Many falling rats.

BEAUTIFUL SOUP

Distinctions end just beyond
that building

across the street,
everything beyond

intense white,
like being in a swimming pool

under a full moon.
It's a beautiful summer

day outside, veil in the air
draped over the trees.

Beautiful women
parting at the prow

of the corner of our apartment.
In their wake, trees flower,

and in the park
behind a hill

still matted where they sat,
a pond blooms

the beautiful green
of soups.

FRAGMENT,
WITH GOLEM

                . . . I get excited and talk
too quickly explaining the river to a woman
wearing mysterious spectacles.
The Moldau meanders through misty fields,
washing the red roots of the willows.
Time slows down around my tongue.
But I haven't had a drink,
I have not altered this golem God gave me
to walk around in. But when I dip a toe
in the Moldau, when I listen to its song
I fall down drunk. My face glows
and fades with the decaying sounds.
I am just a boy beside the river in the pussywillows.
Downstream where it widens
farmers roll up their sleeves and tip back
their beers: the Moldau makes their work go easy.
Their bellies are swelling. Their faces are glowing . . .

THE ROBOTROID
GIRLFRIEND

She crossed the cornscape to see me
in her taped-together vehicle.

Her well-designed nose fit under mine
when we kissed straight on.

Her eyes were glass, she was run-down,
running on residuals.

When she pulled up even the porch swing was asleep.
The Japanese girls were stretched on the floor.

The monster that stole from the fridge
was snug in the cellar.

Her white dress was loose around her breasts.
The pins that held her bare feet on glittered in moonlight.

I laid her on the bed and she kissed me.
I licked her servos, to lubricate them.

I tightened her screws. We hadn't seen each other for weeks —
maybe longer for her, who didn't sleep.

ALTERNATIVES TO PAIN

Then don't think about a fox running around a barn,

he suggested, a small red fox

highstepping through the grass in the dark-grey shade

of a light-grey barn, the day stunningly bright,

the insects stunned and idling.

For days I thought of nothing

but this fox — at night I was horribly buffeted

on an immense game board.

And my little body was a lighthouse of pain.

And it filled with a mean, red heat that was not relieved

by the coloring books delivered to me.

But when I think of this fox now, he does not run around the barn,

he stands utterly still, with one paw raised above the grass,

in a long dark swath of shade. He does not move at all.

Pain is locked away in the barn.

DREAMOCRACY

The most terrifying sound—
an ice cream truck
in the middle of the night.

I'm perfectly flat
feeling my fingerprints.
It occurs to me that
the answer to our childhood questions is:
we're being tortured.

When I'm with my thoughts finally
I'm someone else, I am
driving an ice cream truck through the night
with no lights, pulling on the string that rings the bell.
I am the unwholesome whippoorwill trilling in the moonlight.
I am awake late defending the campsite against elves.
I am a little boy tortured in a sandbox at the army base.
I am throwing sand in a little boy's eyes.
I am getting very sleepy.

HOMAGE TO MY WAITRESS

Skinny girls in the grass

are sipping beer, at the pinnacle

of June, gazing toward autumn.

A skinny one on a blanket bought in Santa Fe

pushes on me, as I push on her, to prove

love is natural. Everything is necessary,

and at higher dosages, deadly.

The sounds of the green and yellow lawn

plow through me —

skinny girls chirping in the grass,

latino radios as usual.

My image in the green pond: is this why she loves me?

Because I have olives for eyes?

She nuzzles me with interest.

I'm shocked by the electricity in her cheek.

I'm so hungry. From somewhere

she produces a long red menu.

STARFISH WAVING
TO ME FROM THE SAND

When I pay close attention to my senses I become immobile.
I'm stuck living each moment
instead of taking great strides across them.
And these are lonely moments.
Without her this desiccated starfish is my only friend,
starfish waving to me from the sand.
Last night an overcoat beckoned to me from the closet.
But that was the whole of our frustrating discussion.
I went back to stare at her portrait by my bed,
to fall asleep and dream of her portrait rippling
on the Ghost Ship's sails.
The rigging creaking was somebody's sighs,
but what kind, and whose?

LIGHT MUSIC

The light music
the sentimental love songs
so familiar
you do not notice them
as they surround you.
You start to cry,
because you will never
be able to demonstrate
that your love for her
is your powersource,
it is a glowing rod in your chest;
because people die
without ever knowing
simple things
about themselves.
When you are turned out
of your home
by the menacing airplanes
what one thing do you carry
with you
that helps you start again?
When you squat
in a roadside ditch
in the shade,
and the sentimental songs
surround you,

where can you run?
And you will have no one
to turn to
for sympathy
among the beleaguered
and filthy battalions
of the Advance Guard.

THE BELLS

It occurred to me — an idea for a new kind of lamp
that changes colors. And just as quickly I dropped it
out the window into the evening.
The sky was dark with enormous cuttlefish,
and cars swished beneath it, and beneath my ears.
It occurred to me — to stand up and fend off the unseen faeries
of melancholy who plagued me,
and twisted up my hair. It occurred to me — to stave in
the motorcyclists' honking heads. It occurred to me —
to shoot at them. It also occurred to me that one of my parts had
    rusted,
that I was like a book you read and only find out after finishing
it that it was about something else, A MENTAL HOSPITAL.

I stood up and brushed the crumbs from me then,
and tinkled.
I felt the impurities leaving me. Memories
also trickled away.
The drops plonked in the toilet bowl like bells.
The bells were ringing for a new day.

FOLKLORE

Moon rises behind my venetian blinds,
in raiments of a bruised, luminous starfish.
There is no power in the air tonight,
a squashed humidity lingers at the bed.
There is no power in a slatted, refracted moon.
There is no power in this heat.
Things that happen just do,
animals dangle in the leaves.
The Moon approaches the window's crucifix
like something rising from the sea, something
that doesn't care if you club it.
But what sort of creature could possibly be indifferent to this?
And why have I already lost interest?

FOLKLORE 2

She says she hurts all over,
but when I lick and assay each piece
we find it's only her heart. Her heart
is sore because her friend has changed
into a bird, and a bird is the most
heartbreaking of all friends
because you can never caress it.
I roll her to her side to assay her ear shell.
The Moon that was crawling behind the venetian blinds
has deserted us. The basil and sage we planted
on the roof crumbled.
The sun rises and retreats
like someone else's pleasure.
My desire is a little cup
with the bottom broken out.

FOLKLORE 3

When the Moon rises it splits the world
in two, each side willing to step over to the other side
to club the teeth out of everyone.

I lie on top of my blankets trying to imagine
that I am these other people I encounter,
pecking from the neck, chortling deeply,
pausing, inscrutably. Pausing. For no reason.
I remain serene on top of my blue duvet,
which is on top of a green fitted sheet,
which is on a mattress,
which is on another mattress,
which rests on the floor of a very large box.
Strings attached to my feet, penis, hands and head
ascend out of the box, into the sky.

FOLKLORE 4

She called him to say they should establish another arbitrary era
the way people always have,
but this one should be based on going to new restaurants.
They both felt Love off the other,
through the little grilles on the phones.
Love made him hungry.
And so did sadness. To lie on the couch thinking
of pawns being shoved through Time
reminded him that Time was working on him
physically too, it was punching him in the neck.
And this made him hungry.
And this reminded him of the autumn dusk of his sixth year,
before dinner was served, and this made him hungry.
And for no other reason did Man divide Time into portions,
than he wanted to grill them, that this would extract
from them their heart's blood.

3

TOMMY'S CAMPING ADVENTURE

I met a man in the woods
who came on strong, badgering
me for cigarettes and news
from the big city. I don't
smoke, and don't read newspapers,
and told him I had nothing
for him. The sky was a bright
inverted pond that leaked down
into the trees, but darkness
rose from the loam, and where we
stood was mostly leafy dark.
A creek crinkled behind us,
whippoorwills said "quick poor will."
"I live in thickets, and sleep
where deer sleep," he explained.
"I can't tell you where that is."

Mornings are beautiful. In
fact, everything's beautiful,
the way we think about things
is bad. I met a man sitting
on a rock, hugging his knees.
He offered me a drink, but
made no move. A bird trilling
was thrilling, it got between
us filling the emptiness
of his offer. I asked him
what bird it was; smiling he
raised up like a shaving mirror
extends, gracefully flapping
his arms. "That was an angel
talking," he said. "They lick me
to sleep." I wanted liquor
intensely, even Three Stills
Whiskey, which made my friend go
blind, and kick out the windows
of the university.

I walked into the sunlight,
leaving the close council of
trees, smelling barley on the breeze.

Rain on the roof is tender
seeming; rain on the tent is
the most peaceful sound. The peace
increased by the flimsiness
above me. I lay in my
tent thinking of my girlfriend,
counting the drops until I
lost count. I counted to twelve.
The rain was a shower of
peace, it kept the animals
hunkered away, and it cleaned
their feces from beneath trees.
The continual plunking
on the canvas extended
interminably, it made
its own time. I was its clock.
I heard footsteps splashing out
in the runnels. A forlorn
hobo sang a song. The rain
washed him away too. It was
impossible in relent-
less assault to remember
the things my girlfriend whispered
to me with her tiny mouth.

In the middle of the woods
stood an unlikely outhouse.
Unlikelier still, the man
inside, humming our anthem.
The trees towered around me
like relatives, the sky was
blue and rushing just above me.
The last time I saw a man
the moon was a red cradle.

He took his time, I bided
mine. I forced a cough. He hummed
more clearly then, through his nose.

Grackles descended to the murky canopy
like sea divers, cautiously.
The insect hum rose higher.

He opened the door inwards
and walked out, eyes first. "Hey there,"
he said. "Hey," I responded.
Then he walked the way I came.
I went inside, and closed my
nose by holding my breath.
The fright I feel for monsters
there will never disappear.

The woman I met scrubbing
potatoes beside the creek
was not beautiful, but was
very tall, asiatic,
and the first woman I'd seen
that month. I stuck out my hand
to greet her; she kept scrubbing
but smiled, and told me her name.
"I'm a racialist," she added.
I did not know what she meant,
but assumed I could still get
what I'd come to get from her.
Only then did I realize
how many potatoes she
had to clean. A pile the size
of a bean-bag chair. That meant
men. I looked upstream: the camp
smoked beneath the canopy
of black, blue-black, green-black leaves.
A whistle, a hound baying:
that was my cue to exit
the tender tableau. "Do you
have aspirin? I'm right in the
middle of an adventure."

4

THE BEST CELEBRATIONS
ARE IN THE FALL

Everyone feels like they're leaving
on a long journey soon.

The blue in the sky is even farther away.

Trucks full of beer
park in the open, they disregard
the shade. The sun is leaving
on a long journey soon.

And the beer is specially brewed
to stay with you
through the cold spell.

And the farmers hang up their tools, they bless the less-to-do.
Stables stacked with straw.
And the aliens they spotted over the silos retreat.
Everyone and all the animals accounted for.

WHAT LIGHT DOES
IN THE FALL

It falls into the sea
minutely, vermilion.
And the fish and shrimp
moving near the surface turn pink
under its glow, and the glimmer of flashbulbs
from the balconies.

There must be a signature somewhere,
some identifying technique, a puzzle
for us on the balconies to see pink and distorted
through our drinks.

The light is pulling away from us, its colors
becoming classical, our rooms becoming more important.
The trees are sighing.
In the summer they might have been whistling, cooing,
but tonight they're sighing.

FALL

The sun goes down but the light never goes,
rain moves through the orange
night but doesn't fall.

The cypresses swell like everything else
in the world and in the air, turning
in cycles.

We are happy and then inexplicably sad

then happy again. Like the clouds
in the sky.

Rain slants across the yard,
over the graves of our lesser pets.
I don't know

if their lives were miserable in their little boxes
or if they just lived,
without news of the world,

until they died. I can see their bones
clearly when I think really hard,
they make a pattern my training hasn't prepared me
    to understand.

AFTER THE WEDDING PARTY

I was involved in a physical act
I was unable to understand
— in love, but also walking back
to the dining car on a train going 80 miles an hour.
I strongly believed Truth was a fixed point
in the trees, watching me travel
through the southern nightfall
backwards, recklessly. I misunderstood.
My lover cradled a camera
to her weakened eyes,
to take a picture of where the night just was.
Common decency forbade me
from expressing my love
down her shirt under the mothering eye
of a town's watertower.
The tower said "Smile America"
and "I plugged Heather Griggs."

YOUR BOOK

Strangers came into the apartment
walked right to the bookshelf
to spill beer on your book.

Your book on a hook dangling off the roof
attracted a white horse to the door.

Your book emitted physical waves
into the air, drying my hair.

You climbed a tree to write
your book where you wouldn't be seen.
There was no tree there
until you made it.

The shimmering leaves seemed to be powered by light.
The tree shuffled this light into strings.
The strings hung from the air.
The printers sewed your book together with them.

63

THE NEW WINE

I stole two bottles of wine from work
and my boss will never read this.

One, the new wine, a red shirt
hanging among suits.

The other, a nosebleed
scrubbed by a mother after school.

They may be gifts. If we love this new wine tonight
will we still love each other?

If I pour it in the humidifier will the flies
fall drunk on our faces?

Will the new wine make us young?
Will the creepy DJ play
monastic voices again
when we make love by the light of the computer?

Will you lower your blue body to the wooden floor

again, as when the dove looked in
and monastic voices sang the wine to sleep in its new sacks,
our bellies?

WITH MY FRIEND'S COMPOUND BOW

I shot an arrow at a wooden fence
— it went through a hole
with the illusion of being drawn
to something it already knew
in the field beyond.
Late orange light behind everything.
Stove agape. Three shoes.
Dirt path worn by men,
but not a shortcut,
no signs of hurry.

Violence felt shiny and clean,
and physically repugnant.
I felt my arms as they really were—
alive beside me.

I cannot say anything with certainty
about my friend except:
he had a filthy, open fish pond in his living room;
a Cockateel's guano accumulated on his dresser.
But his thoughts were like icebergs to me.

The arrow could have killed someone,
instead it disappeared.

And nothing happened, it remained
dusk a while longer.
And the next day, nothing.
Then one day my friend stabbed me in the arm with a pencil.

THE RETURN OF THE GIRL

I always thought I would be dignified
when I saw her again.
Not rubbing my rough chin in my usual shoes.
Not standing in a corner of an antique store
fingering political buttons of the opposition.
Not relying on the shelving unit to hold me up.

Oh I placed my hand there so carefully so frequently.
It was a wonderful shelf, really, full of objects
that needed scouring and out-of-print red books.

Her new husband's black hair seemed plastered to his head;
that look of youth and health.
I stared at his hair instead of her breasts.
Something kept me from looking at them
with an historical perspective:
a powerful flu remedy.

I was too busy swallowing.

And noticing all the clocks running at different times,
all the paperweights with their sour inertia.
All the women with hairdos

in the shapes of great nests
and more brains.

SEARCH FOR EXTRATERRESTRIAL INTELLIGENCE

I'm writing upside down with the space pen,
listening to the rain.
My wife is writing about the Black Death
and its effects on Art, and asks me
"Where are your pants?"
They are on the floor in front
of our new couch, where I arranged them
to spell out L-O-V-E. A vegetable,
mystic thrill runs through me —
the couch is something's antenna. It bears
good love to us here over the laundromat.

I'm waiting for the Light Beings
to remove my roof.
Our bedroom is lousy with clothes
spelling out greetings if anyone's up there
who can read English.

WHEN DISTANCE
BEGAN

I was investigating a woman smoking
a cigarette privately
from the last train car. Basically
she was in Italy and I was in Paris,
though we'd just kissed.
Distance had never been understood
until the train pulled away,
we believed there was no world beyond us
till we made it.
But there were always cows
or something there,
bales of straw.

I'd followed the woman for a month, coming
to understand her. That orange jacket
haunted me from every closet later.
Wine in a bandshell.
Champagne in the river.
But our parting glass drained my will to live
and broke my mind into functional units
that time couldn't pass between,
I had no way of seeing from point A

to this penne with spinach and mascarpone.

LIKE THE BACK
OF A STAR

A perverted scenario raises its tail.
I'm emitting strings.
And drinking whiskey.
Unconnected facts lie dead
on the table. A star burns by the window,
and when I close my eyes I want to see something
like the back of a star,
but there is a street-lit bedroom in there,
a bedwarmed smell leaking from underneath.
Disembodied smile tilted among the pillows.
Rain ruling the windows. Sounds,
vanishing and unidentified. But I expect to hear them
again when I step off the surface of this planet
and make my way purposefully to the next one.

CUTTING THROUGH
THE DARK

I saw a superlative blue in the sky
over the park tonight, on the other side of dusk,

and what sense is there in description?
I will never tell you how blue.

You will never look up at six o'clock in February
to see it shimmering behind the park

and think of me. Things sidereal and black flapped
above me not like bats or birds,

like nothing that ever touched down.
Night was immense and cold,

it tilted, it slipped down.
The savant bums did not ply their chess.

The boards were empty like dreams of the future.
No one sold me drugs.

Simply the essential came to pass,
I moved like a stiff toy dressed in blue.

Horseplay was far away, though a horse stomped
under the monument, a cop horse.

COMET

We could hitch the Horses of Instruction

Twice I heard them under the window

Under our flophouse, lousy with towels

Stamping under a moon

How many moons have circled our leaking heads and hearts?

One

The same one every night, hitched to the Horses of Instruction

It's a heavy heart they drag through the hills

My heart sinks into the couch

Yours into the sink

We believe Love lives in the heart

Which goes in and out

Why did they teach us that?

We want to pin it to a constant

Let's pin it to a comet

It'll return

OKLAHOMA

I awoke in the parking lot at the lake
staring up at the fireflies
and the sneer on the moon.

It was so late my brain was stupefied
and if I had been a character in "Peter and the Wolf"
I would have been the tuning fork.
The smells peeling off the lake were glassy, elusive —
for the most part putrid, with hints of hyacinth

and on the blacktop was a baby carriage.
The baby was plastic but who's to say
it didn't conceal a real baby inside it,
wondering through weighted eyelids?
It's spooky, they have their own little world
where they still travel by carriage.

MY GOVERNMENT

The history of the world
is the history of rural malcontents
rising up against the capital.

Each night I hear something scratching
to get in my fortress
which can only hold out so long.

The cat thinks something lives in the radiator
and puts his mouth to the vent — its breath.

No man is an island. Also, no one is interested
in excessive indeterminacy. The French
will eat the horse right out from under you. That,
and so much more, have you taught me, World.

Your products will collapse after a short time
and we will be forced into the streets for more.

It is possible to live only on what you grow yourself
if you eat little and lie very still.

YES

I ate a Morning Glory and turned
yellow on the inside. The garden smelled
like quince, pungent quince, ringed
with white stones. There was a yellow light
on in my insides but it couldn't come out,
not through my waxy ears
or the slit in my underwear.
I balked. I ate a Poppy, which symbolizes artfulness
but also sleepiness
and forgetting
and I fell supine below the quince, among
the jettisoned quince. In this state
I was hyper-sensitized.
I was the planet's nipple and let me tell you:
there was no love anywhere except my own.

And my mind was a tabula rasa, I think.

MOCKINGBIRDS

Mockingbirds mastered police sirens
and now the city is on edge.
Grinding their teeth at night, the people
send out their swollen moans to the powerlines.
Their dreams are troubled: a caravan of trolls
bedding down, picking their yellow teeth
with a white chip of bone.

The people are no less uneasy in the morning rain,
when no birds sing. When lumpy blue clouds
gather outside like flies' eyes.
When a house is pounded by rain and for the first time they hear
how small it really is

FROM THE WORLD AT NIGHT

I went out one night with people from work

to an editor's apartment. I drank

a glass of poison. She served me poison

and everyone else was either immune

or politely refused. In the subway

I didn't know the meanings of any words

and my sweat stung me. People on the car

pushed me off at the next stop when I puked

in my hands. Without any meaning, time

accreted to things in funny shapes — old,

asymmetrical hobbledehoys

tormented me, a stern but benevolent

lizard gave me counsel. My stomach contents

spilled around me. My mind was actually

seven or eight minds, all but one of them

composed of helicopters. The other one

was sad. Satellites could tell I was sad.

When another subway came I crawled on

and technically I passed into death, but

passed through and awoke at Coney Island

and saw black cowboys galloping on the beach.

Hungry, mentally defeated, I stared

at The World's Largest Rat — for fifty cents.

Really, it was only the same color

as a rat. "It's from the same family,"

the barker explained. I felt vulnerable

illuminated by neon and fried light.

Everyone had to use one big toilet

and the sky was orange with satellites.

And satellites know everything.

FROM THE WORLD AT NIGHT

I was five, sleeping in the creepy room

where my great grandmother died, years before.

All I knew about her was a convex

oval daguerreotype. Others said she

had been cruel and quiet, and was a ghost.

That room was never comfortable.

Something woke me one night: the house felt empty.

I was scared in the dark halls, my ears hurt.

I passed the huge humidifier

and saw the front door open, my grandparents

standing on the cement porch with their arms

at their sides. Across the highway, cornsilk

reflected the moon. Joining them on the porch, they didn't

look at me or make a noise. A small cloud,

bulgy, brown, and yellow, hovered above

the corn. It came closer.

No one ever talked.

from SONNETS TO MAYHEM

Riot in Ann Arbor

A very drunk man shimmied upside-down
on the wire holding up the traffic
light, to do something terrible to it.
Even beautiful girls took such delight
warping private property out of shape.
Your Gold Dress played in a cupola, fire
finished off the upside-down cars, Chef Jan's
restaurant cracked under the pressure. Todd
and I stood inside a murderous crowd.
They were eating rodents right off the ground.
Windows kept up a crashing, like cymbals.
If our team hadn't just won "Greatest Team
Ever" it would have been a desperate waste.
We would have been embarrassed to tell you.

The Bullet

The bullet bit his shoulder blade and sailed
from his shirt, vanishing into uselessness.
In recovery he dreamed of passing
a hamlet in Indiana, where this
bullet was born, in childhood's Oldsmobile.
In the dream his father parked the huge car
by a small yellow house; an old woman
showed them the cellar where her husband bent
forks and spoons into bullets. "Here's your fork,"
the man said, shoving it into a gun.

The doctors let him out in the cornflower light,
winter settled in, the trees in arrears.
Now there was an eighth gate to his temple;
what woman would be the eighth gate keeper?

THE ELF

On top of a hill in the park I found a ruined fort,
graffiti and the low-lying, lingering smell of old urine in the dirt.
Inside an elf lay on his side, with a splint on his leg,
and small silver pistol by his head. His black hair was matted
    with sweat
and he stared wildly past me, never focusing on me,
but addressing an idea he had of who I must be,
shouting "Three wishes! Now you must grant me three wishes!"
I backed out, "uh," I said, blessing him in this way,
and hurried back down the matted path to the Great Lawn
where some kids played baseball, and magpies
soared and dove in the air. I felt like I knew them personally.
The distance between the birds and the prosthetic lenses on
    my eyes
was almost fifty yards. The distance between the birds and
    my spirit
was nothing, I walked on, squawking.

GLIDING TOWARD
THE LAMPS

The way a woman keeps her house
makes me want to sleep over
to see how she comports herself alone.

I see from across the street this woman likes to snuggle:
her alcove is smothered in comforters.
I imagine being curled up in there against the wall,
watching her tonguing a cruller.

As I glide home I think of the Robotroid Girlfriend,
and I am gliding toward the little lamps in her eyes.

I have turned her every-which-way and never
found the fuse box. I don't know how she works.
I think of the way she lies rumpled
in the rumpled bed, everything inside her switched on
    and purring.

I would love her bare arms to scissor my neck again.

NIGHT ON CAPE HATTERAS

Tart air sweeps off the sea in eddies I map with smoke.
At night the house fills with a presence shaped like a house,

something about to happen; things open and close
in other rooms; a cellar door inside me opens;

we have to get out of bed to look in the closets
to confront our fright before it spoils our dreams.

The smoke is taken from me, sucked off the porch.
Soughing ever upwards, to die.

It is brave of me to use that word *sough*
that makes me curdle.

The curtains fall like snowdrops on the slopes of her eyes.
At night the rain seeks our valuables. As we seek each others'.

BROOKLYN BRIDGE

Bowlegged lady crawled across the river on cables,
and towers above me, sinuous stone lady.

Below me nothing but the two-inch dimension
of the two-by-fours, and birds bugging the barges.

Her graceful pelvis arches into the orange evening,
implaccably. Who is she waiting for?

CREDO

I believe there is something else

entirely going on but no single
person can ever know it,
so we fall in love.

It could also be true that what we use
everyday to open cans was something
much nobler, that we'll never recognize.

I believe the woman sleeping beside me
doesn't care about what's going on
outside, and her body is warm
with trust
which is a great beginning.

MATTHEW ROHRER was born in 1970 in Ann Arbor, Michigan, and grew up in Oklahoma. He attended the Iowa Writers' Workshop, University College Dublin, and the University of Michigan, where he received the Avery Hopwood Award for poetry. His first book, *A Hummock in the Malookas*, was selected by Mary Oliver for the 1994 National Poetry Series, and published by W. W. Norton & Co. It was also selected by *Publishers Weekly* as a Best Book of 1995. Matthew Rohrer has had many fulfilling jobs as a janitor, lab animal caretaker, cook, and alphabetizer. Now he lives in Brooklyn and is a poetry editor for *FENCE* magazine.

Designed and composed December, 2000, by Neko Buildings
Text is set in Filosofia, designed in 1996 by Zuzanna Licko of Emigre
Display is set in Template Gothic, designed by Barry Deck in 1990
Printed by Thomson-Shore on acid-free, recycled paper